PILGRIM'S BUMPY FLI

T0143333

Pilgrim is a little plane who loves flying through the sky and zooming through big hoops with their friends. At home, however, Pilgrim experiences frightening behaviour from Jumbo, who represents the perpetrating parent, that makes them feel scared and sad. Pilgrim is comforted and guided by Jet, who represents the victim/survivor parent, to think about safety and what to do when frightening things are happening.

The trauma a young child may experience from domestic abuse can impact their entire developing system, making them feel worried, frightened, and unsafe. Safety planning is an essential component of direct work with children, offering a way to help them vocalise their feelings and understand what to do when something does not feel right, and this storybook is a key vessel for communication and exploration. The story, which is rhyming and engaging, enables young children to engage in the narrative in a non-threatening way. This book aims to be accessible to all children from all families where safety planning is needed as such the characters in it are non-gendered.

This beautifully illustrated storybook is a crucial tool for the early years sector, education staff and those working in children's services, including safeguarding officers, family support workers, social workers and children's Independent Domestic Abuse Advisors/Advocates IDVAs. This book is designed to be used alongside the companion guidebook, *Domestic Abuse Safety Planning with Young Children: A Professional Guide*. Both books should be used in tandem with agency policy, procedure and guidance.

Catherine Lawler is a qualified specialist children's counsellor, trauma practitioner and childhood survivor of domestic abuse and coercive control. She has extensive experience working with children, young people, adult survivors and families as well as developing and facilitating training on the issues of domestic abuse and coercive control.

Nicky Armstrong, B.A.(Hons) Theatre Design, M.A. Slade School of Fine Arts, has illustrated 30 books which have been translated and published in 7 countries. She has achieved major commissions in both mural and fine art painting.

Pilgrim's Bumpy Flight

Catherine Lawler

Illustrated by Nicky Armstrong

Routledge
Taylor & Francis Group

LONDON AND NEW YORK

Designed cover image: Nicky Armstrong

First published 2024
by Routledge
4 Park Square, Milton Park, Abingdon, Oxon OX14 4RN

and by Routledge
605 Third Avenue, New York, NY 10158

Routledge is an imprint of the Taylor & Francis Group, an informa business

© 2024 Catherine Lawler and Nicky Armstrong

British Library Cataloguing-in-Publication Data
A catalogue record for this book is available from the British Library

ISBN: 978-1-032-36529-9 (pbk)
ISBN: 978-1-003-33286-2 (ebk)

DOI: 10.4324/b23172

Typeset in Bembo
by Deanta Global Publishing Services, Chennai, India

This book is dedicated to my brother. He is a kind, caring, thoughtful and respectful gentleman. Love you little bro.

This is the story of Pilgrim the plane

I wonder if you're thinking, "that's an interesting name".

Pilgrims fly here and there

This little Pilgrim flies everywhere.

Pilgrim the plane loves to fly

Up, up and away into the sky.

Loop the loop, round and round

Then safely landing on the ground.

Pilgrim goes to flight school with other little planes

Where teachers help them learn and they play games.

They fly over land and over sea

Until it is time to go home for tea.

After tea it is bath and bed

Time to lay a sleepy head.

Getting lots of rest for the next day

So, Pilgrim and friends can learn and play.

Whooshing in the sky, doing loop the loop

Zooming with friends through giant hoops.

But some days the hoops feel small, and
Pilgrim doesn't want to fly at all.
The hoops feel small when Jumbo gets mad
Making Pilgrim feel scared and sad.

Jumbo would growl like a big grizzly bear

Giving Pilgrim such a scare.

Jet could see Pilgrim was scared and sad

Jet felt the same when Jumbo got mad.

So, Jet taught Pilgrim something new

They talked about it while they flew.

"If your heart feels like it's going bum bum bum,

Or you get a horrid feeling in your tum.

It's your brain telling your body you're having a scare

Your brain's very clever that's why it's there".

Sometimes Pilgrim's brain would click into gear

Thinking I don't like what I see, I don't like what I hear.

Pilgrim's brain was a clever place

It was trying to work out how to keep Pilgrim safe.

Should I fly away?

Should I hide?

Should I run to Jet?

Pilgrim couldn't decide.

Jet said, "Let's think what to do when Jumbo gets mad,

When your heart goes bum bum, and you feel sad".

They thought about where Pilgrim could go at

home, out of the way

Who Pilgrim could talk to now or the very next day.

19

These ideas are called a keep safe plan

Try and remember them if you can.